Familiar History

poems by

Guiseppe Getto

Finishing Line Press
Georgetown, Kentucky

Familiar History

Copyright © 2016 by Guiseppe Getto
ISBN 978-1-63534-043-3 First Edition
All rights reserved under International and Pan-American Copyright Conventions.
No part of this book may be reproduced in any manner whatsoever without written permission from the publisher, except in the case of brief quotations embodied in critical articles and reviews.

ACKNOWLEDGMENTS

I would like to thank all the people and places that inspired these poems, who are far too numerous to mention, as well as the literary magazines kind enough to print versions of some of them, including:

Gloom Cupboard – "Burning Wishes"
Reed – "Black Earth"
Slant – "Borderlines I Have Known," "The Zen of Death and Dying," "Winter Technologies"
Redactions – "Anthropology"
Eclectica – "Familiar History" (as "The Perimeter of History") and "Crazy"
Sugar House Review – "On the Banks of Forgetting"

I would also like to thank all the mentors over the years who helped me make these poems as good as they are. Mrs. J. Adams, my first grade teacher, was the first person to call me a poet; may she R.I.P. Gailmarie Pahmeier first introduced me to the art of literary poetry and first told me I had some talent in it. Connie Hales taught me what a professional poet's life holds and how to develop an aesthetic all my own. I'd also like to thank Jessica for her love, support, and patience during the crazy-making process that is poetry writing, including reading many a draft of a terrible poem that thank everything will never see the light of day.

Publisher: Leah Maines

Editor: Christen Kincaid

Cover Art: Rebecca Woods-Baker

Author Photo: Guiseppe Getto

Cover Design: Guiseppe Getto

Printed in the USA on acid-free paper.
Order online: www.finishinglinepress.com
also available on amazon.com

Author inquiries and mail orders:
Finishing Line Press
P. O. Box 1626
Georgetown, Kentucky 40324
U. S. A.

Table of Contents

Winter Technologies 1
Hunger Signification 3
Borderlines I Have Known 4
On the Banks of Forgetting 6
Anthropology 7
Burning Wishes 8
Black Earth 9
Surely Some Revelation Is at Hand 10
Airline Technica 11
Agricultural 12
Separated at the Supermarket 13
Destroyer 15
Familiar History 16
Gaming 19
Crazy 20
Intergothic 22
Certain Light 23
Waiting for Rain 25
The Zen of Death and Dying 26
Operation Costs 27
Thankskilling 29
Rid 30

To all the desperate lives left waiting

Winter Technologies

Snow falling within the beam
of a streetlight as pixie dust.
The river is intransitive.
Black. Boolean. Midwestern.
Its facets are moving at the same rate
as that which would overtake you.
The thing you lost. Young.
There was a river then, too.
And ice still chunked and waiting.

It's the same song playin'
Everywhere I go.
How many hands laid end over end
make a horse? Floes of frost like
sequins in the coat. Dry flakes.
Polyester. Curry comb. Moonlight.
No one knows where you are
right now. You remember the story
of the father from a school paperback
who fell through the ice drunk
alongside bare branches. Must've
been these. Yours is undetectable
because you're out ninja-ing
in the sharp intake of corrals again.

This story means something different
every telling. Brake lights turn
from the first stackyard, flash twice,
go silent. There is no creaking
of springs. No soft white thud.
That's your imagination working.
Snow crunches in the creak of rubber.
Working. The herd still standing
in its steaming mess.
The bowels obstruct nothing yet.

Nowhere to go but the horizon
Where then will I call my home?
CD changers aren't hatched yet,
much less MP3. Neither is freeway,
hatchback, humid, doctorate, instant replay,
teenaged rubbers scratched out
of the cement ground
for their scent by coyotes.
The past is a homunculus that bends
its knees and breathes a whisper.

Hunger Signification

The dark flash of killdeer crying
into the dirt shoulder
is set to repeat through the basin,
miles more than I'd like to see.
Ohh, can't anybody see
The tight whine of sung syllables
break the syntax of the crouch
of mountains, and the storm
rocks the truck bed back and forth,
directionless. Telephone wire.

Guardrails stay rust.
Circuitous. What happens
when the rearview mirror
sends back something unexpected?
Copper beeches. Hay hauling.
Musk of her morning scent.
Working myself up and the tires whine,
jump forward into anywhere but here.
Static is breaking itself up again
from the speaker wire come loose.
Windshield wipers.
We've got a war to fight

This town. Population 143 and count
the fourth wall missing,
the gray brick schoolhouse.
Field this time into the transformer.
It blows and sparks rain.
There is a child walking nearby
and caught away
from his mother's reach he reels
right into the dusk
emptiness nuzzling up
against foothills.

Borderlines I Have Known

First there was me, of course. A dark sun. Squatting in the corner of the house I grew up in. In the front room lit only by a single red-brown bulb entwined within an adjustable sconce connected to a lamp stem that went to the ceiling. Maybe that was all the sky I saw for some time. My mother took pictures of me in the mint leaves out back. Maybe I split first like a rhizome or a zygote. Tripling in density hour by hour, breath by breath. My mother used to lay newspapers down all around the house for me to shit on. I was four. The same year I declared I wasn't going to get any older because I didn't want to become my father, or at least this is the story I was told until I forgot the real one. The midway point before I learned that the brain records everything, especially when it is told every morning to forget every night.

Granite scars, given enough pressure, enough time. And then the only way to trace history is by following lines that go back farther than blood. Into black. A scientist once removed every part of a cat's brain except the basic drive motors. The second borderline had black hair and eyes and wore black often. And red. In the summer her skin was the color of blown brown glass. Back when I learned that fucking produces a kind of suture between two bodies. I still remember the jagged footsteps she was taking when I found her wandering through the neighbors' flower garden in a blue blanket. From my gray pickup with the black flames she looked so white and small framed against what passed for winter in California.

Maybe the third point of contact was mountains clearly visible. Smog only a picture-window distortion. Bodies moving under the blur of snow pack receding year by year. Mountain shadow. Maybe where you couldn't step in the alkali skims, liquid pockets that looked so dirt-like, was where I could've found my center of gravity. Maybe had I run in circles fast enough in the trailer park where I should've ended up, I could've developed fascination with the ground sufficient to keep me off thin ice. I used to dream about a man like the riptide of a black hole, who came out from the house I grew up in into the backyard where I was at night and I rebounded from him like his field of vision was the wrong polarity. One night my mother woke to me in full seizure in the bed we shared, the one my father left empty for me, and she tried to pry my jaws apart with two fingers, which you must never do to someone that conductive. One day I fell slowly on the playground, sure I'd been clotheslined by one of my classmates, and woke to the static of white gravel in that awful sun and then it never happened again.

On the Banks of Forgetting

Women where I'm from were caged by Jesus. In 1995, as my neighbor drove her minivan beside the canal, some young punk with a black mohawk mooned her from one of the spillways, his white buttocks refracted by the moss-green water. In spring, before it was hot enough, the water pulled by current sucked us into it even standing on the bank looking at our blurred selves looking back. The canal was dredged in 1916 by horse and pulley, long after Joseph Smith had declared this continent filled with His other sheep. I always wondered if his disciples arrived here suspended somewhere between the shelf of wind and low-hanging clouds, the ones that always sent me digging for old movies I'd seen fifty million times. Old was 1986. In 1916 it was spring, too, but sound came in low, refracted mercilessly in the cottonwoods. The Indians called them *leafshakers*. The heat-ribbed dirt waiting for asphalt to ripen and rip its own skin along the path the canal would take. The path I would take, touching the bare leg of Nicole under the water with my toe. Trying to say *a fish* right, but it never coming out right, and her just staring down and past me at her own reflection. Past the cow pasture, and Nicole's house, the pain skips on the surface of remembering what happened. I dripped on the carpet watching the green spark of Patriot missiles on television. My mother told me to go dry off but I wouldn't yet. Instead I would bang my elbows into the edges that didn't fit, the light glancing low and fatal at the corners of the window in my bedroom and outside the hammock twisting, its reflection caught in cousin Nadine's window. Does that wind still exist? Does it falter up the faded blue rims of mountains or the syllables that left no impression? The angles of shadows the shakers cast, why do they come back? A stone skipped in a dream state that won't go straight because dusk is twisting outside again. My father is watching *The Dead Pool* in the living room, which has nothing to do with water. His feet twitch when he sleeps and that reminds me of never seeing him that peaceful again, of twitching my toe beneath Nicole's black eyes, of forgetting.

Anthropology

Words fall short, the second teacher ends.
Her raised platform is the color of salmon
split open from gorging on red clay,
her robe the color of overcast sky.
Beneath short-cropped black hair,
just a few flecks of gray,
black eyes burn across the distance
from body to body, synapse to response.
I shift in my cross-legged position
and the buckwheat imprisoned
in my black cushion sifts like grain
once whispered from the auger
amid all that engine noise—too many years ago.
The heavy pine door thumps twice
each time it's opened—a heart drum.
I frown, *what's left?* The wood falls
from its carefully stacked position
by the cast iron stove and from within
a cinder rises in an arc toward the surface,
kuh-chuk. I turn my head.
Ten billion years. *What do you notice?*
The teacher asks. I answer in my mind,
though I'm not supposed to: concrete,
snowfall, glint, bedrock, white, white.
Outside the air sifts fine, winter
slow as glacial shift.

Burning Wishes

The rains have come again, out of the canyon vertex
of interstate and commuter suburbs.
Reaching for edges of the glacial cut valley,
granite cliffs press inward, outward, downward,
limey-gray, holding gravity for the aerial view,
spring, summer, fall, winter, and spring.

Tree roots hang from the rim of the gorge.
And if the meadow near the cutting
is the best campsite, it'll be filled with people, guaranteed.
How tadpoles are born into a dying lake, just to turn belly up
and slime slowly into whatever first starlight
traveled farthest to reach us tonight,
is another story.

Someone said they never saw a wild thing
sorry for itself. Me neither, but it seemed sometimes
like they ought to be. The bark beetles that crunch
in and out of their white fir tunnels
and branch outward until each thorax, leg,
and instinct intersects, becoming a web
meaning nothing.

A cold snap couples indeterminately with wind velocity
and the fracture lines of ice particles, killing only incidentally.
And apparently when a trail is called a shuttle, it's because
you can't get home on your own, back to where
Slide Mountain's melt water-soaked shoulder sloughed off,
roaring down Ophir Creek Canyon clear to the highway
eighteen years ago.

Down in the valley someone is cheating on me, my Lord,
Kumbaya, but I will toss each lit match into the wet fire pit,
hoping. What else is there after years of echoes?
After a forest outstrips even its own pathology?

Black Earth
   -For Jessica and Kanaalaq

In the muck under a snowbank
in the Woldumar preserve, slippery spring.
I fell after balancing precariously,
even with the horizonline for half a breath,
laughing, my hip bone drawn like the edge
of thaw toward its source. Two miles in
on the bridge over the Cedar River,
your golden-brown hair listed over your white
and blue nylon carapace. Wispy flakes began
to flurry one by one. *Where now?* We looped
back to the rebuilt barn, the ancestral cabin, once,
my fault for bragging I knew directionless sky
and quaking ash better than street signs.
Paw prints and I said fox. Probably somebody's beagle.
We were running, but not into cliché. Somebody
with more guts had stood on thin ice at the pond's edge,
and the whole time I kept thinking
about the same snowglare only rimming
an empty parking lot. At the gate the poster
in the store said *Owl Hoot* or *All Crawl* next Sunday,
the office volunteers politely ignoring
our fogged-up stares. The same flux of information,
just a different channel. White noise. Silence.
The creak of thaw or bootsteps. What difference
does decay make? If I were to wait here,
on a hundred and seventy-eight acre ranch
given back, skirting the frozen wetlands
and waiting for the return of game,
could I return? What umbilical gets broken
in the quest for fire? Before we crossed back over
the dividing line, a cedar fence gone to rot
and split in its middle by new white pickets,
you said something asymmetrical considering
the weather had gotten into your shoes,
something like: *I like the snow because it tells you
which way the wind is blowing.*

Surely Some Revelation Is at Hand

The door clicks open; enter crunch of dirt,
Arms squared. Feel like this want, driven.
Senses dragged by spruce ashes,
The closest neighbors that can't see
Hillside or sky left days ago. The dam, motionless,
Heralds fall, teeters on the edge of uncertainty,
Burns timelines down to a nub.
Not because of entrails; not because

Of what happens next. From across the spillway,
Based on the best of judgment, and southwest,
Maybe thirty or so degrees, the fire fighters' plane
Scooped that diver from the lake.
He suffocated in the tank, they think.
His remains, like a falling cross, only marked
Absence, spindled down into this season,
A created color, desperate for inertia,
And the deep flute of pine branches.
Centrifugal forces always seek a center,
The observer, a point of reference.
The first to wake to the flickering light
Traces the ecliptic on the bedroom wall,
And calls *fire, fire, fire.*

Airline Technica

First altitude, dizzying stomach, cramps.
Then cheap cups sweat. Red eye
Or feels like. I wake violently to my own
Numb right hand clutching my left.
The 9-year-old woman-child two seats over
Drops a non-dairy creamer packet,
Breaks the unspoken armistice against
Reaching over total strangers. Her tiny hand
Steadying her rests nonchalantly on my thigh.
The wisps of her dirty blonde hair
Are my cousin Nadine's, lashed next to me
In a suicidally-maintained Dodge caravan,
My rumbling right thigh vibrating desperately
Against her left. *The way things have changed,*
My headphones jibe. The woman-child
Retreats, the non-dairy creamer belonging
Nowhere. Where is her mother?
Perhaps arriving home from bookkeeping
A trucking company to find us "playing"
Beneath the *no smoking* light,
A crazy ex-Green Beret
Who puts cigarettes out on his tongue
Her idea of a babysitter.
Maybe ice-fragged window glass
Is the only thing separating her
From certain adulthood, the modular carpet
Of Rocky-ridged clouds the distance
From child to parent. I suppose sending
Your kid on a solo flight is nothing compared
To the time Brian Whitlock and I
Painted armor on ourselves
With spray-on cattle disinfectant we found
Beneath the old steer chute.
We're headed west to east, which after all these years
Still feels like going up the downslope.
During descent, flecks of incontrovertible light
Dust sun motes above the backward thatch of fields.

Agricultural

First, the starlings will take flight,
rippling like twists of dark
into the horizon on which they balance.
The tension of wind breaks west
where the highroad had washed out years earlier.
Near flattened tires that hold down brown stems
of the hayleage pit you could smell for miles
a hand had pissed on the electric fence
out of sheer stupidity or the need
to feel touched by fire from the inside out.

My father compares the scream
to a sparrow caught in a fan belt. Mud-caked,
he breaks in his wobbling gait from the diversion ditch,
from where he couldn't have heard,
unless the wind caught the sound and carried it
over a mile. From fields gone fallow
for years, I trudge uphill, sinking clear
to my socks in alkaline dirt,
and squint into the same sun, remembering
only the way he took the man's hands
to lift him gently from the billowing dust.

Years later, I find my father in the loader
filling in the drain ditch at the north end,
and past him the alien slopes covered in sawgrass
and no house yet. My mother
tells me it's *a bridge to get to his concubine*
and not to water the lawn.
In the fields, alfalfa makes its long green rope
behind the swather, and ducks
circle toward the riverbank as the blades eat their nests.
Behind him in the cab in the noise and heat,
I wait for either of us to say anything.

Separated at the Supermarket

In the parking lot this isn't the truck I remember
we gave to Aunt Desolina, yellow, 1979,
a Mazda, the clutch went out when I was seventeen,
the driver's side door handle never worked.
The sun in the shopping carts has its own
sort of smog-centered drain that beats down
into the junkyard I buried my first dog in
beneath a little cross made from garden stakes.
There was always water a few miles ahead
on the highway that went anywhere but here.
The pale light is digging in again. The entrance
arches into it, orange and white. *Winco.* At least
reach through the heat of her against you
in the mountains to cement, each step.
Dig in with your toes the way that kid
took a shit and buried it with his own foot
in the sandbox behind the guest house, was he related?
The pecky cedar-fenced dog pens, the cat
in the air conditioner belt that just kept yowling
no matter how many mommies leave their carts
and babies staring beside the endless soup cans
into the space that reads pine nut hunting,
or the empty pallets left by every Friday night
I never wanted. Come back. What absolves me
from buying every kind of toothpaste, her scent,
I don't remember, I'm forgetting why I came here,
to my father putting his fist through the upstairs window.
The body is a broken relief. I haven't
even made it past the cucumbers,
or wading knee deep into drainage water
so mites can wade knee deep into the blank
white snow lines that mirror, in her eyes,
already fading, everyone on gravelly blacktop
spinning around me, careful not to touch,

everyone trying to get to the center,
where everything is processed. One baby in particular,
don't look at it. In the milk aisle. In the semester
before fucking for the first time. Its eyes the color
after the rains before that black window
in the irrigation ditch fastens itself to Hope Valley.
The horizonline is making everything smaller
than it really is. I never could work somewhere
this washed out. I pack everything wrong:
motor oil and salami, first thaw before
we came back from winter waiting for us,
the too bright sweep of X-mas cars reaching
into the black.

Destroyer

Down into the gravel pit near the fence that intersects
the wall, I think a creature that sits and eats and waits.
There is nothing there of course. My mother is telling me
something at the kitchen table I don't want to hear,
something I want to block from the tracking device

of my memory. Hard to recollect what has been knitted badly
like a scar. Fake wood grains in the paneling, the wall inside
is like the wall outside: a confinement zone, a teenage
holding pen. In formation, cousin Nadine marches in,
bearing goldfish crackers and a puzzle missing a few pieces.

The eye of the horse or blossom of the Japanese Spindle Tree.
Euonymus japonicus. Spike-thorn family. It will die badly
near the gravel pit, in the soil where not much grows,
in the shadow of about six desert winters, and the puzzle
will stop matching altogether outside of a few fading pieces.

I think a grassy knoll outside the window
that is not a window, a shooter that will execute on sight.
I put him on a ten count while my mother breathes heavily,
sighs, continues. The sun is setting.
The psychotropic bullet spins a bleak, wide path

through her voice, hits me, lower abdomen,
like a bolt of surprise dawning.
My mother looks happy, because she thinks for once
I am surprised by what she has to say.
The damage is electric. It ranges outward from the pelvic floor.
That way I can't remember whatever happens next.

Familiar History

Growing up in a place like this is like
growing up on the moon. I want to picture
the second house exactly so that I will know
what to tell you—clean, clear lines like an evergreen forest.
The stale air in the living room. The dust
exchanges. The world on the wall
according to my dead grandmother: a skunk
disappearing into a log in a dark aspen grove
whose painted leaves, upon close inspection,
are tiny flames.

Out from that aluminum siding moves skyward.
The foundation is crumbling. Everywhere
putrid green except where flames ate
a chunk away on the east side and then
mysteriously were satisfied. Another weed fire
took the power lines that used to run
from the telephone pole to the shop.
Insulation thin and stale with dry rot.
Spiders everywhere. Objects in relation
to each other become the same.

Out back my cousin Tracy is about to hang
a rooster from the swing set and then
beat it to death before sunset, but why before
sunset? What happens then? What if
he lets it live? Something will hunker down
inside him. Something will want out.
I will learn to seal everything up inside.
We all will. In 1969 the desert will swallow
an atom bomb whole. In 1969
my grandmother's pancreas will swallow
too much of the awful light from a safe distance
inside a bus. After awhile you begin
to realize light in the desert can penetrate

anything. A 1951 description
of the Nevada Test Site, included in an Army brochure
for the Camp Desert Rock soldiers,
tells them that the desert is *a damned good place
for disposing of used razor blades.*
It is.

This is the space without my father.
Don't try to fill it with anything else.
When it rained into the corn and dust,
he used to say it was like a cow pissing
on a flat rock. It was. My mother read
romance novels to me while I was still
in the womb. I can picture the words
echoing from flesh the size of the walls
of the Lunar Crater. The Lunar Crater
is a maar.

A maar is formed by the heating
of subterranean water. Or, in other words,
it is nothing. It is something
they tell you so you won't believe
the sky can ever burn. It is something
they put you on a bus and drive you
into the middle of nowhere to see.
It is something to help you fall asleep
at night under the skeletal fingers
of poplars that keep erasing stars.
It is used in the sense of *don't worry,
nothing can get through the maar.*
Or it will bring you uncontaminated
ground water. Or it will bring back the stars
from 1969.

In 1963, a limited test ban treaty
was signed by the United States
and Russia, which means the tests
went underground. From here on
history becomes a dotted line.
Why would my grandmother get on a bus to see
what was miles beneath her? Why would
she feed her pancreas processions of invisible light?
In 1969 my mother graduated high school.
In 1969 Michael Collins, Command Module Pilot
for the Apollo 11 mission, ended 21 days
of quarantine by saying *I want out.*

Gaming

Sun bleaches cumulonimbus.
The pressure change blunts engine sound
Like going under water. Cliffs,
The Colorado River like a branch schematic,
And beneath where no warning
Could dissuade weekend warriors,
Rivulets of mercurial gray. Service tray.
You will away the attendant's eye,
Ice-pale, and zirconium looped hot
Through one auburn lock, imagined
Driving smile-first into a perfect
White. Maneuvering
Anklebones with the grace
Of an apothecary, her hips measure
Pull and thrust. Turbulence
Rattles the overhead compartments,
Dormant streetlights below
The color of waiting matchsticks.
Not even tree-house-tree
Planned far enough to barely register
Commuter suburbs
Can sate the need for human flavor,
For salt and stink. Terrible coffee
Next door takes shape in Styrofoam
Like the hiss of a weapon
Finally holstered. She turns,
Eyelashes bending to every
Programmed demand.

Crazy

My old high school surrounded by its sea
of sun-bleached pasture grass. In the hallway
there's a crack in the lime green paint
tunneling toward the attic, where all
the dead bodies of students nobody'd miss
wait for some honors student
who knows too much to find them.
I'm leaned against the wall with Jill Summers.
She puts headphones over my ears without warning,
and I hear Kurt Cobain for the first time,
singing *well I swear that I don't have a gun.*
I do. In that instant I look back to see her chin-length
brunette hair fall over her jawline. Her left ring finger
brushes my head when she takes them off.
I replay that moment over and over again
later, sweating under my sheets.

My mother in no more than gray summer light
drops an omelet on the floor and it comes up coated
in dog hair, cat hair, and god knows what else.
She scoops it up with her other hand, slaps it
on the plate and puts it down in front of me,
saying nothing. I become fascinated by the rim
where flowers reach from muck of the past.
Irises, I think. I know this because my mother
fancies me a gardener. I stay up
late at night to watch softcore porn on Cinemax,
the next day hazing into hours of watering
her butternut squash, my pumpkins she reminds me
I've planted since I was little, her marigolds, her roses,
her irises. All the desperate lives left waiting.

Richard Hugo says you write the same poem again and again.
I read this for the first time after bucking hay
out back of the feed store, sky darkening toward snow.
Someone taps the counter with their index finger and I look up
to see my own sixteen year-old self staring angrily back.
Does that make me crazy?

Intergothic

Enter cities. Now it is the winter solstice;
now the fixed savior's birth. The sky
burns gray. White. And between
the coming days, freezing rains
spat from faces crooning crudely down
frame hours that murmur and shriek
through crowds. From steel and glass,
electric numbers tick out
looking for something warm,
something fleece that packs easy.
Pigeons swoop and scatter;
hearing strains to parse the clack
of soles on marble reading floors,
the sputtering of faux-leatherbound pages
that tell us why things don't fall down.
It actually is all to do with how the forces act
within the structure, & keeping the direction
of the thrust within the wall by loading the top.
Direction and the weight of bodies hold us.
From the travel section, fingernails
like amber tick over the ancient mausoleums,
the statues in the square. Soon,
the appended complaint of ancient trusses;
soon, the highly indexed
five centuries-long decline.

Certain Light

The cornyard in back of Mackedon's
Cement is a real cornyard on real cement;
her hair is really barley sifted from the auger.
I like guys who walk with Him, she says,
and whatever draws your eye from hers
draws crooked railroad cars all sporting
the exact same manufacturer mark.
Forty-seven degrees south by southwest,
your father, now a geothermal power plant technician,
burns more whiskey most nights than rock.
From the first skeins of frost
in tire ruts, stickerweeds and days like this
drain on the baseboards of the shacks
on the westernmost edge. Now.

The blackened ruins of an ancient chicken coop
across from the first house
that your mother, the pyromaniac, burnt down
while roasting weeds. A two-story farmhouse
corralling distant relatives.
She doesn't admit the way her husband looks
at their boy, not even to herself.
Everyone here becomes one family anyway.
Same cottonwoods that flake from the char.
Same faded cotton dress embroidered
with tiny sunflowers. She wonders
when her life slowed to an old movie poster,
headlining the day she saw you from the highway,
your ear pressed to the railroad tracks
that translate the wind's hum from Hazen,
which is four houses and an H spilled
in white feldspar on the hillside behind.

Then. Turn from the gravel driveway one last time,
her tiny house across the canal
too dark to differentiate overgrown crab grass
from the flint emptiness of sky.
Try to write your way out of dust devils
that spin apart at the seams, the chunk of
pink granite forty miles due east
that marks grandma's dirt body
fine as cigarette ash. They'll etch deeper
line by line the way a diminishing lake
leaves its traces on a mountain.

Waiting for Rain

Clay banks sigh white dust without relief.
1978. My father drifts in an aluminum boat
on a bottomless lake, gaze rippling
to the edge of depth, where blue falters green.
Algae lists; the fishing rod jerks.
He opens something inside himself and waits.

After keeping books and phone calls
ten hours a day, from the woman on shore
clutching her gold windbreaker tighter
against grit and wind blear a single mother
will wake to tell the story of meteors
that carved the two halves of Greater
and Lesser Soda Lake, of divers
who plunged deeper and deeper into grainy darkness
for years, finally succumbing to the grief inevitable
when natural laws are broken.

The worst time my father drifted, weeks settled in
like salt. After his usual morning whiskey
with a dash of coffee, he'd decided to pick rocks
from the roller mill with his bare hand. Beer helped,
as did long silent days. Beyond the pecky-cedar fence
the milk truck rolled in and out, its men extending the long hose
into the barn receptacle. Mud puddles thinned
back into memory. In the dark of the living room
we waited for new skin to grow, for blood to fade
from the roller mill, the TV shimmering
like a fish belly. Afternoons died hard
and heat came stirring but never waned.
It was then I learned to fold against myself upstairs
in my single bed across from where my father slept,
to prop my head in the windowsill,
watching the sky unfold gray within gray.

The Zen of Death and Dying

Out past etched white salt flats
in the open ranges the dead brush
grids moonlight, spotlight
less than secondhand in what's left.
Wind strays in after registered
movement. Tracking without
prospect. I unwind like an impossible
sunlight trajectory from under
a wool blanket in the bed
of the pickup to find cold
distance gleaming back. Cloud-striated stars.
When I tell him I don't want to do it
because the sky is watching, my first
cousin's mullet-haired boy friend
will look at me hard from whooping
to say *beautiful*.

Years later on my way back to the ranch
I see one on the highway in its
dark red life and go back to check.
Not static enough. Thunderheads that night
bring down power lines across from
the front pasture and next morning magpies
descend like heliotropic snowflakes.
Christmas Eve falls on no trace
of the last cord connecting
stimulus to stimulus or nights swept
clean. Before any of that
I'll lean close to the long, still ears
in case they still conduct somewhere
and whisper *doesn't that feel good?*
Snow has already begun to fall.
Noon is gray. The clouds, hanging,
snuff out everything.

Operation Costs

History frequently loses nighthawks
angling like sonar pinging canyon walls
fletched with rain shear. Range
from which night spins up and out,
due north. Forty-five degrees
of squatting in the dank,
under and behind the coming,
John Muir crested the ridge above
the basin in 1875
to find Hyde's sawmill
booming like a bad ghost.

No sounds similar
is what the forecast says.
Standing, why not seek shelter
like every other thing
living, warm-blooded or not?
An infant's four hundred foot shadow
caught over the collar bone,
the strange urge to bow,
thirty-six degrees the threshold
for writing b*ark-strewn forest carpet floor*
and words wished said

when she handed back the ring,
business-like,
just a tiny spark forged
in unmistakable pressure down
where heat gives no light
or sign of reference.
Malingering. The stomach begins
to quake, giardiasis, or wake
tonight to the garbled bird call,

expecting the face no one sees
or some other minor demon
staring upside down beneath
stark white aspen fingers,

and fumble with the flashlight to find
only a Daddy Longlegs resting
on the shoulder. Thirty-six degrees
of getting it wrong all the time. How.
Walking the way out, this meadow.
An adult can drink as much
as 137,000 gallons per growing season.
One theory is that the water table shifted.
Now the young get swamped early.
When Hyde gutted the ancestors
and left their stumps to bleach out here,

the senses change nothing.
The stiff grass felt prickly to feel the damp.
What sound did the ancestors make
to fall like forest whales,
killing any potential profit
with their own wrong weight?

Thankskilling

The vandals are fretting through the leftovers
Again, I hear them. One borderline personality
Wears gathering like a collar. Another
Tangles in the couch cushions on mescaline
And Tanqueray. My father, the self-medicating
Bipolar, wafts in faking a hip-hop limp,
One three-fingered fist gripping a Budweiser,
His other hand cupping and throwing
An imaginary fart, riddling *why niggers don't think
Their farts stink*. A cup of violence spills
From the neighbor lady's shift under the table.
Her lags speak shards. The bombs headed to Afghanistan
Bleed something awful for days, squeaking
Like chew toys every time I open my fool mouth.
The average annual Afghan income of 800 US dollars
Is unimpressive to neighbor lady. *They should
Start their own businesses, selling sand*, she declaims.
One of the meth mouths from Section 8
Calls Grandmamma a cunt, proceeds to shatter
The other's (his mother's) car window with his fist
On his trek back to town. All I can think
As meth momma blubbers *whyyyyyyy* over the peach cobbler
And instant coffee is how long will she hold onto
Her last, defiantly pearly, white? I watch it sleeping there
Beneath the event horizon of her shiny red gums
Until I realize now this is just a terrible story
I can tell at slightly more sane parties.

Rid

At first he was lost. There were browning animal bones everywhere in the detritus: ribs, digits, even a vertebra or two. The breeze felt strange; the rains hadn't come, but the fog had lifted from the valley, and, rimming fir trees dug in at elevation, the postcard lake. At last a bird which had come here to die told him where he was: the wind like static, mountain shadow, ancestral spring. He was six years old deer hunting with his father.

As he approached the bird, he saw it wasn't dying at all. Snow patches crunching beneath his boots made a rubbery squeak, each step. He imagined the sound as an interruption in a long cone of silence extending westward clear to the edge of the preserve, where the cutting breaks into runoff come March. *Forget it*, he could hear his father saying. *The bird is gone.* His rifle butt touched the ground as he squatted down near it, now in range of its tiny, wheezing breaths.

The bird's eyes darted frantically from black to dark gray and back. *A wren. Or thrush.* His father was terrible at identifying birds. Or trees. Or pretty much anything living. Or dead. As he stood up he remembered that his father was blind drunk, anyway, if this was the time his horse untied itself and wandered clear to the interstate. By now the screech of twisting metal had boomed down a nearby ravine like the snap of a rifle report. The bird was startled, of course, joined as it was to the metabolism of other lives, but until they rose, it could not rise either.

Guiseppe Getto is a Zen Buddhist, a poet, and an Assistant Professor of English at East Carolina University. *Familiar History* is his first chapbook. His individual poems can be found in journals such as *Sugarhouse Review, Slant, Reed, Eclectica, Santa Clara Review,* and *Redactions,* among others. Though poetry is definitely an avocation for him at this point, he has been writing poetry most of his life. Like many writers, he uses art to process a difficult upbringing. He was born and raised in rural Nevada, a landscape littered with nuclear fallout from above ground atomic testing, violent cowboys, and dysfunctional family systems, including his own. This landscape is largely the palette he continues to use in most of his work even though he has lived outside of it for many years now. He currently lives in North Carolina with his wife Jessica and their cat Jackie. There is far less nuclear fallout in North Carolina and the cowboys are milder, but there are about the same amount of dysfunctional family systems. Visit Guiseppe online at: http://guiseppegetto.com/poetry.

www.ingramcontent.com/pod-product-compliance
Lightning Source LLC
LaVergne TN
LVHW041506070426
835507LV00012B/1369